Little Pebble™

## Our Pets

# Hamsters

by Lisa J. Amstutz

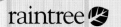

raintree

a Capstone company — publishers for children

Raintree is an imprint of Capstone Global Library Limited, a company incorporated in England and Wales having its registered office at 264 Banbury Road, Oxford, OX2 7DY – Registered company number: 6695582

**www.raintree.co.uk**
myorders@raintree.co.uk

Edited by Marissa Kirkman
Designed by Juliette Peters (cover) and Charmaine Whitman (interior)
Picture research by Morgan Walters
Production by Laura Manthe
Originated by Capstone Global Library Limited
Printed and bound in India

ISBN 978 1 4747 5713 3  (hardback)
22  21  20  19  18
10 9 8 7 6 5 4 3 2 1

ISBN 978 1 4747 5426 2  (paperback)
23  22  21  20  19  18
10 9 8 7 6 5 4 3 2 1

**British Library Cataloguing in Publication Data**
A full catalogue record for this book is available from the British Library.

**Acknowledgements**
We would like to thank the following for permission to reproduce photographs: Alamy: Barrie Watts, 17; iStockphoto: DeirdreRusk, top 9; Shutterstock: ANKorr, top 15, asife, bottom 7, dwori, 21, Emilia Stasiak, left back cover, IgorAleks, 5, Karen H. Ilagan, bottom 9, katfox.art, top 7, LIUSHENGFILM, bottom 15, Mr Aesthetics, (wood) design element throughout, Natalia7, middle right back cover, PhotoStock-Israel, Cover, SAHAN SVITLANA, 13, stock_shot, 19, tanya_morozz, bottom 11, 20, Tsekhmister, middle back cover, Vyaseleva Elena, middle left back cover, ZaZa Studio, right back cover, zilber42, 1, top 11

Every effort has been made to contact copyright holders of material reproduced in this book. Any omissions will be rectified in subsequent printings if notice is given to the publisher.

All the Internet addresses (URLs) given in this book were valid at the time of going to press. However, due to the dynamic nature of the Internet, some addresses may have changed, or sites may have changed or ceased to exist since publication. While the author and publisher regret any inconvenience this may cause readers, no responsibility for any such changes can be accepted by either the author or the publisher.

# Contents

# Listen!

Squeak!

What does this hamster want?

Maybe it wants a treat!

# All about hamsters

Hamster fur is soft.

It can be long or short.

The fur can be many colours.

It can have spots.

A hamster can fit in your hand.

It has a short tail and legs.

Look! It has small eyes
and ears.

**Chomp!**

Hamsters chew a lot.
This stops their teeth
getting too long.

Hamsters can not see well.

They use their noses
to find their way.
**Sniff!**

**Dig!** Hamsters dig burrows.

They make nests there.

**Zzzz!** They sleep in their nests.

# Growing up

Baby hamsters are called pups.
They drink milk from their mum.

Four weeks pass.

Now the pups can eat

seeds and nuts.

They stuff food in their cheeks.

They store it for later.

# Playful pets

It's night-time.

Hamsters play.

They run in wheels.

They hide in tubes.

**Peek!**

# Glossary

**burrow** tunnel or hole made or used by an animal

**chomp** to chew

**fur** thick hair that covers an animal

**nest** place to sleep, have babies and bring up young

**pup** young of hamsters and some other animals

**sniff** to breathe in quickly through the nose

**store** to save or put away; hamsters store food to eat later

# Read more

*Hamsters: Questions and Answers* (Pet Questions and Answers), Christina Mia Gardeski (Capstone Press, 2017)

*How to Look After Your Hamster: A Practical Guide to Caring For Your Pet, In Step-By-Step Photographs*, David Alderton (Armadillo Books, 2013)

*Nibble's Guide to Caring for Your Hamster* (Pets' Guides), Anita Ganeri (Raintree, 2014)

# Websites

www.bbc.co.uk/cbeebies/topics/pets
Discover a variety of pets, play pet games and watch pet videos on this fun BBC website.

www.bluecross.org.uk
Find out more about how to choose a pet and care for your pet on the Blue Cross website.

# Comprehension questions

1. What time of day do hamsters play most?

2. What are baby hamsters called?

3. Would you like to own a hamster? Why or why not?

# Index